SCIENTISTS WHO STUDY
THE EARTH

Mel Higginson

The Rourke Corporation, Inc.
Vero Beach, Florida 32964

© 1994 The Rourke Corporation, Inc.

All rights reserved. No part of this book
may be reproduced or utilized in any form
or by any means, electronic or mechanical
including photocopying, recording or by
any information storage and retrieval
system without permission in writing from
the publisher.

Edited by Sandra A. Robinson

PHOTO CREDITS
© Mel Higginson: title page, page 4; courtesy U.S. Geological
Survey: pages 10, 12, 13, 17; courtesy Ocean Drilling Program,
Texas A & M University: pages 8, 15, 18; courtesy AMOCO
Corporation: cover, page 7

Library of Congress Cataloging-in-Publication Data

Higginson, Mel, 1942-
    Scientists who study the earth / by Mel Higginson.
      p.   cm. — (Scientists)
    Includes index.
    ISBN 0-86593-372-3
    1. Geologists—Juvenile literature.   2. Geology—Vocational
guidance—Juvenile literature. [1. Geologists.   2. Geology—
Vocational guidance.   3. Occupations.   4. Vocational guidance.]
I. Title. II. Series: Higginson, Mel, 1942-   Scientists.
QE34.H54   1994
550'.92—dc20   94-7000
                                                        CIP
                                                         AC

Printed in the USA

TABLE OF CONTENTS

SCIENTISTS WHO STUDY THE EARTH

The Earth isn't alive the way a robin or squirrel is. However, the Earth rumbles, shakes, coughs fire and is always changing. Studying the Earth is a fascinating job.

The people who study the Earth are **geologists,** or Earth scientists. They study soil and rocks, mountains and canyons, oceans and streams. They also study the powerful forces that cause earthquakes and volcanoes.

Earth scientists study the underground forces that create natural jets of hot water called geysers

WHAT EARTH SCIENTISTS DO

Like other scientists, Earth scientists look for answers to questions. Earth scientists easily answer some questions: What kind of rock is this? Is this really gold?

Other questions are more difficult: When will the next earthquake happen? How was the Earth formed?

Earth scientists work at answering questions by adding new discoveries to what other scientists have already learned. They also use a variety of tools and instruments, from hammers to computers.

An Earth scientist takes a rock sample that may show a coal deposit

KINDS OF EARTH SCIENTISTS

The family of Earth scientists is large. Some choose to study oceans as their special job. Others study the huge, frozen rivers of ice called **glaciers.**

Some Earth scientists are interested mainly in the past. They want to know how and when the Earth was formed. They work closely with scientists who study ancient animal remains, called **fossils.**

One group of Earth scientists studies rocks from outer space — **meteorites.**

These geologists work on a ship and study undersea soil and rock that they bring to the surface

WHERE EARTH SCIENTISTS WORK

Earth scientists work in offices, **laboratories** and outdoors — "in the field."

Field geologists search for oil, natural gas, gold and other valuable materials in the Earth.

Being an Earth scientist can be exciting, but dangerous, work. They sometimes crawl into caves and underground mines. They may also work underwater.

Earth scientists sample gases from cracks in the Earth near a volcano

Earth scientists visit Mount St. Helens' field of lightweight volcanic rock called pumice

Two scientists (lower left) inspect a forest destroyed by the explosion of Mount St. Helens

THE IMPORTANCE OF EARTH SCIENTISTS

Understanding the Earth and the forces that shape it is important to everyone. Earth scientists help people find valuable metals and fuels. They help locate coal, natural gas, oil and underground water.

Earth scientists help people know more about the Earth's ancient past.

By learning about earthquakes and volcanoes, Earth scientists can warn people before a disaster occurs.

Aboard the ship JOIDES Resolution, scientists drill deep in the sea floor to gather samples of rock and soil

STUDYING VOLCANOES

Geologists who study volcanoes see some of the Earth's greatest natural forces at work. However, studying live volcanoes is risky.

In early 1980, Mount St. Helens began to hiss and rumble in Washington state. Mount St. Helens exploded with great energy on May 18, 1980. Geologist David Johnston, who was six miles away, died from the volcano's poisonous gases.

Mount St. Helens' explosion on May 18, 1980, sent up clouds of poisonous gases

DISCOVERIES BY EARTH SCIENTISTS

Each day, Earth scientists make discoveries around the world. The more places they visit and study, the more they learn about the Earth.

Some scientific "discoveries" lead to **theories.** Theories are ideas that make sense but cannot be proven.

An important theory of Earth scientists is that the **continents** — Earth's huge masses — move. That theory helps Earth scientists understand events such as earthquakes.

Scientists study deep sea soil samples to find out more about things like volcanoes, earthquakes and mountains

LEARNING TO BE AN EARTH SCIENTIST

Earth scientists have a deep curiosity and interest in the makeup of the Earth.

As young students they begin to learn about rocks, minerals, oceans and land forms. In college they study the sciences, especially Earth sciences.

Many Earth scientists continue college studies after earning a four-year degree.

Earth scientists prepare for careers that sometimes take them close to the fiery eruptions of volcanoes

CAREERS FOR EARTH SCIENTISTS

College prepares Earth scientists for many special jobs. Many Earth scientists are hired by private companies to look for valuable underground materials, like natural gas and copper.

Many other Earth scientists work for universities and governments. The United States Geological Survey hires geologists — nearly 1,500 of them!

Glossary

continent (KAHN tin ent) — any one of the seven great land masses on Earth, for example *North America* or *Africa*

geologist (gee AHL uh gist) — a scientist who studies rocks, minerals, earthquakes, volcanoes, oceans and land forms

fossil (FAH suhl) — the ancient remains of plants and animals

glacier (GLAY shur) — a massive river of ice

laboratory (LAB rah tor ee) — a place where scientists can experiment and test their ideas

meteorite (ME tee er ite) — a rock from outer space that lands on Earth

theory (THEER ee) — an idea most people agree with that explains why certain events take place

INDEX